I WAS BORN ABOUT 10,000 YEARS AGO

A TALL TALE RETOLD AND ILLUSTRATED BY

STEVEN KELLOGG

Morrow Junior Books
New York

Colored inks, watercolors, and acrylics were used for the full-color illustrations. The text type is 14-point Palatino.

Copyright © 1996 by Steven Kellogg

Printed in the United States of America.

2 3 4 5 6 7 8 9 10

Library of Congress Cataloging-in-Publication Data
Kellogg, Steven.
I was born about 10,000 years ago: a tall tale / retold and illustrated by Steven Kellogg.
p. cm.
Summary: Born about 100 centuries ago, the narrator has seen many things happen since he watched Adam and Eve eat an apple.
ISBN 0-688-13411-4 (trade)—ISBN 0-688-13412-2 (library) [1. Tall tales. 2. Humorous stories. 3. Stories in rhyme.]
I. Title. II. Title: I was born about ten thousand years ago. PZ8.3.K33Iam 1996 [E]—dc20 95-35079 CIP AC

For the two heroic Colins, with love

AUTHOR'S NOTE

In *Huckleberry Finn,* Mark Twain's greatest novel, the hero accuses his creator of having told "some stretchers." Telling stretchers—elasticizing the truth and peppering it with humor—was indeed standard practice in nineteenth-century American storytelling. Whenever yarn spinners gathered, a spirit of good-natured one-upmanship led to bouts of boasting and outrageous exaggeration that gave birth to many a tall tale. *I Was Born about 10,000 Years Ago,* in which the narrator boldly injects himself into various biblical and historical settings, with improbable and humorous results, springs from that period. The tall-tale spirit of a century ago continues, inviting all of us to unfetter our imaginations and let them soar.

I was born about ten thousand years ago,
And there's nothing in the world that I don't know.

I saw King Pharaoh's daughter
Fishing Moses from the water,

And I'll lick the guy who says it isn't so.

I saw Satan when he looked the garden o'er,

I saw Eve and Adam driven from the door,
And from the bushes peeping,
Saw the apple they'd been eating,

And I swear that I'm the one who ate the core.

I taught Samson how to use his mighty hands,

Showed Columbus how to reach this happy land,

And for Pharaoh's little kiddies
I built all the pyramiddies

HAPPY BIRTHDAY CHEOPS

And to Sahara carried all the sand.

Queen Elizabeth she fell in love with me,
We were married in Milwaukee secretly,

But when sneezing overtook her

I went off with General Hooker

A-shootin' skeeters down in Tennessee.

When attacked once by a raging dinosaur,

I said to him, "Why snarl and rant and roar?
You've been misunderstood.
Deep inside you're kind and good."

It was clear he'd never heard these words before.

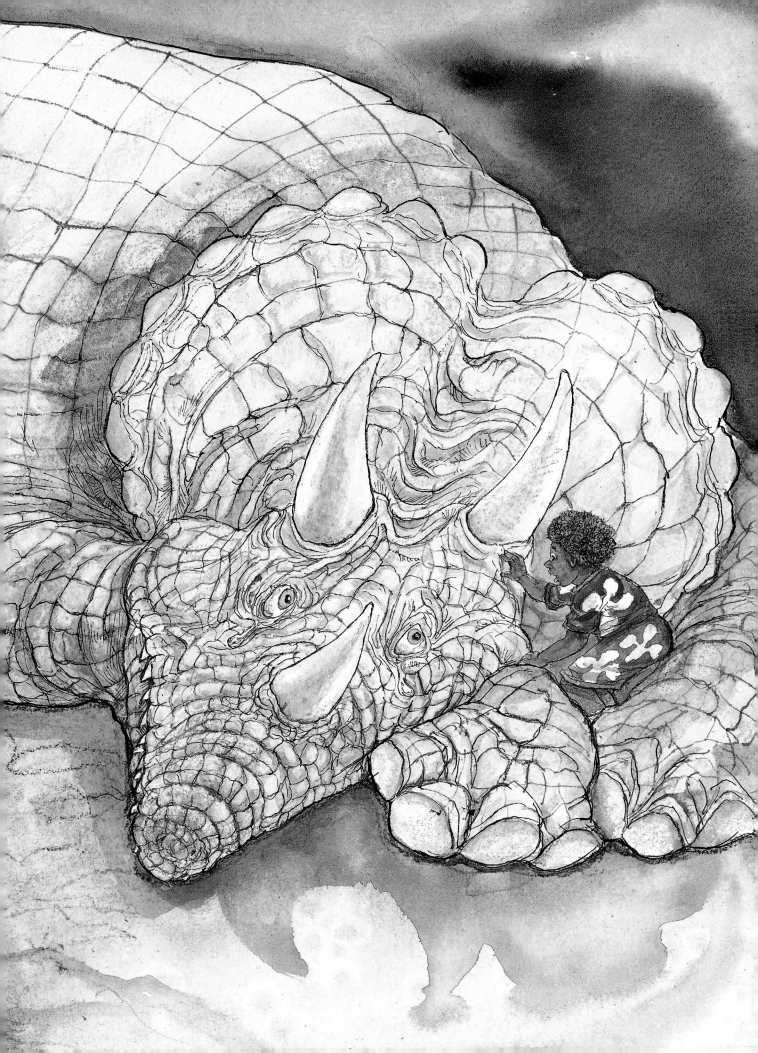

When Paul Bunyan called for loggers I was there.

I helped Johnny plant each apple seed with care.

Pecos Bill and I drove cattle

Clear from Texas to Seattle,

Where I taught Mike Fink to wrestle grizzly bears.

I played hopscotch with some spacemen on the moon,

And I plan to visit Saturn very soon.

But first I'll need a rocket,
And a lot of food to stock it,

Since I won't be back till school gets out next June.

We've stretched the truth a bit, but now we're through.
The next tall tale will have to come from you.
Putting whoppers into rhyme
Was the way folks passed the time
For about a million years, or maybe two!

ACHOO

I WAS BORN ABOUT 10,000 YEARS AGO

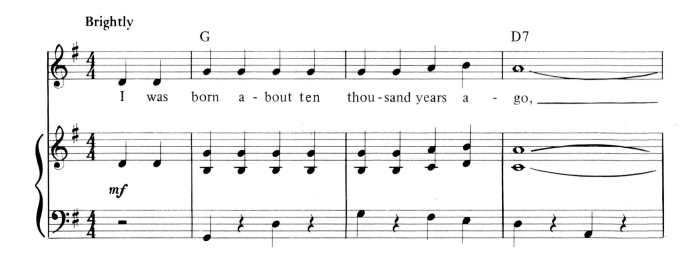

I was born a - bout ten thou - sand years a - go,

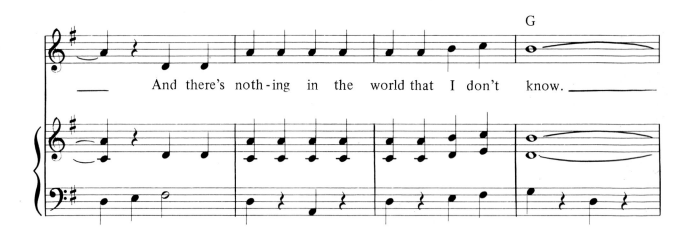

And there's noth - ing in the world that I don't know.